How Not To Give a Shit:

The Art of Not Caring!

Jack N. Raven

Jack N. Raven

No part of this book may be reproduced or transmitted in any form whatsoever, electronic, or mechanical, including photocopying, recording, or by any informational storage or retrieval system without express permission from the author.

Copyright © 2013 Jack N. Raven Publishing Company

All rights reserved.

ISBN-13:
978-1495254178

ISBN-10:
1495254178

Table of Contents

TABLE OF CONTENTS 3

INTRODUCTIONS 5

SURVIVAL AND REPLICATION VALUES 5

EMOTIONAL DISCHARGING 8

CHANGING MINDSETS 10

ABUNDANCE MENTALITY 11
A DASH OF SUPERIORITY COMPLEX 12
THE PSYCHOPATH 14
WILLPOWER 14

NOT CREATED EQUAL 16

PLEASING OTHERS FOR THE SAKE OF PLEASING 16

WORLD REALITIES VERSUS YOUR OWN REALITY 17
PERSONAL BUBBLE 18

THE BUFFERZONE 19

SOCIAL CONDITIONING 21
KNOW THYSELF 21

WHY DO YOU CARE AGAIN? 23

Jack N. Raven

EGO 25

EGO FEEDING FRENZY 25

SELF-ESTEEM VERSUS EGO 26

CONCLUSIONS 27

OTHER BOOKS BY JACK N. RAVEN PUBLISHING

Introductions

the purpose of this book is to give you the tools or the off-switch, when necessary to prevent you from caring too much! There is inherent power in being a psychopath as it were, of not being too emotionally invested and operating with more logic and control of over our primal instincts and emotional urges.

The true professional!

The ideal is to achieve the power inherent with the natural psychopaths while retaining our humanities. To have full control of our emotions, be in touch with them without being enslaved.

This book contains tools to make you understand why we care too much, that it incapacitates or hampers our performances, preventing us from maximizing our potentials and getting the job done.

What I did in this book is lay out a minefield so you can navigate them better. Better understanding of the nature of the beast (The Carebear lol), will allow you to tame it.

It is my goal that by the end of this book you'll have something to practice out in the real world. That you'd have installed an OFF switch in your mind that will let you turn off the caring mechanism should you desire it.

Survival and Replication values

In evolutionary psychology there are only two things important in life. Survival and Replication. Survival is anything that helps you survive and increase the quality of life. This could be money, properties, social alliances, power etc. Having lots of material potential allows you to increase your survival quotient. Some like the above increase both S and R values!

Replication value is anything that will allow you to spread your genes! Having gorgeous face and body, creates attraction within us because they are health indicators they make good mates who'll improve our genetic pools and produce healthy off-springs!
Almost anything in life can be reduced to these 2 values. We emotionally react to anything that threatens or can quite possibly may improve it. And to stop caring is to stop reacting! A hot chick passes by, you probably can't help but check her out and feel aroused! The prospect of making lots of money makes some of us excited. Anything that threatens to take them away, creates the opposite emotional reaction within us.

All in all at the very core a lot of it is just due to Survival and Replication values plus things that may affect our egos in some fashion. Anything that doesn't directly affect the S&R but damages our self-esteem and self-image is an example of caring due to ego issues which is another matter. At time it can get tricky not knowing if the influence comes from the unconscious mind or the ego/pride.

Receiving credit for a job well done, without seeking recognition is completely different from someone doing things entirely for the purpose of getting their egos stroked! That is ego influenced caring. Suppose someone is doing his best, completely committed to closing that multi-million dollar transaction, is that merely pride or trying to improve his financial holdings? Survival value increase if he succeeds in closing that deal after all.

How about those lame guys we constantly hear about, no self-respect left, he does everything the girl thinks she wants, and anything that he believes will impress her? All to no avail, he still gets rejected, disrespected and hurt, but spew he trudges on! If he succeeds? That's replication value for him!

It is never good to solely decide on courses of action you'll take for the praises you'll get. Even if you succeed you are still supplicating or living in reaction to people like a puppet! You are still trying to validate your self worth by how others react to you! Self-worth and core self-esteem comes from knowing your real values regardless of others contrarian opinions.

For one reason or another let's say for political gains you may need to gain people's favor, empathy, respect and validation-which are valid reasons in this case to seek it! In this sort of situation you are no longer doing it to feed your ego but for actual material gains.

Although they may seem identical-trying to get validation from people and getting their approval etc. they are not identical. One is entirely concerned and perhaps care too much of what other people are thinking and saying. The politician or the tactician on the other hand only cares because of the actual, tangible, material benefits it will give him!
He couldn't care less what they think of him personally as long as it gets the job done and gets the desired results!

He's not surrendering his power nor self-worth or value to the opinion of others He may care what they think AS A WHOLE, for political gains but on a personal level? He just doesn't give a flying fuck!

If you are not careful you can get stuck in the same routines doing things for the glory and the praises instead of the actual tangible benefits from those courses of action. It is this very same addiction that could later on take its toll on you because you are doing things in supplication without realizing it. Who really is in control of you? Are you doing it for you or for other's reactions?

Supplication is caring too much what they think that everything you do is motivated one way or another by their opinions! It is a position of lameness or weakness to go through life just wanting to impress everyone in your life! Be naturally impressive and they'll get impressed, but don't do it because you care of what they think and want to impress-big difference! Do things for you and the benefits, not because they're going to stroke your ego.

There is inherently nothing wrong with people naturally being impressed by your accomplishments ; consequently receiving credit where it's due. Many, perhaps too many don't realize they're becoming enslaved by external validation. Thinking they are in command of their lives but deep down actually just want the approval and validations coming from their peers.

It's a Catch-22 trap or a vicious cycle which can get addicting if we don't hold it in check.
Music to our years whenever we get good compliments and praises. We want more of anything good! If we don't? It sucks so bad we need to get our next fix from the next thing! A vicious cycle indeed.

Emotional Discharging

Sometimes it is not enough to change your values and internal programmings to stop caring or giving a shit. You may need to manually manipulate the feelings and discharge the emotions. In order to do that you can employ NLP, hypnosis but the more preferred tools are either Sedona method or EFT (Emotional Freedom Technique). They are designed specifically for that purpose: discharge emotions. The metaphor which could explain how this works is that underneath, structures and roots make up the emotions.

By chopping down on the root causes of emotions, you can from the ground up minimize or completely eliminate the entire emotional energies powering it-thus disabling and rendering it impotent.

Some problems can only be fixed by emotionally and energetically discharging or chopping down the roots of the problems, not merely eliminating the symptoms-not even addressing the problem logically!

Others require more and need the rebuilding of the internal programs that make it up. For the most part it is beneficial to combine techniques.
Discharge & Reprogram the mental and emotional programs and influences from the inside-out.

How does it feel?

The feeling of being emotionally discharged in that manner is conceptually it's still there, but the feelings are nulled. Like you've gotten a shot of lidocaine, totally numb to the emotion.
With some emotional issues, that may not enough as with the case of approach anxiety and similar problems.

For instance you can do all sorts of energy discharging work and make the approach anxiety completely disappear and yet that person will still have problems approaching women, though he doesn't feel the anxieties anymore!

Why is this? This particular problem, and not all problems are the same, need to be reprogrammed not just emotionally discharged. Intellectually perhaps more motivations should come in the form of carrots and sticks would have to be installed there. The same goes for reprogramming someone to stop caring of rejections or what a target or prospect would think of him. Due to his mental programmings he's gotten accustomed to seeking validation from everyone's so merely discharging it will also not be enough.

New thinking habits have to be formed and incorporated to adopt the new, ideal outcomes.

If that is not enough you can of course just use Will power to aid you but that is not a good long-term strategy. You can only hack things up to a certain extent; until you get exhausted and give up. It's not a good long-term strategy. You have to find more energetically efficient ways to install the new and ideal behaviors and desired outcomes!

Changing Mindsets

Another approach you may want to check out is how you can make yourself organically not care! One way to do this is by making people expendable! Well not really, but learn to perceive them as such.

It's such a nifty and convenient power to have whenever you need the feeling and power of abundance and would like to relegate the annoyance of caring too much. If you care too much of that one thing? Imagine you literally had 500 as backup? Would you care as much if at all?

And you can play that game as long as you know how to approach and make an unlimited number of prospects- anytime, anywhere!

Salespeople have been doing it for ages! It's not a big deal, they can do what ever, buy them or not I don't care because I know it's a numbers game! Some will, some won't, who

cares?
Imagine the power and flexibility, and the lack of neediness if they're just expendable!

A lot of these ladies men appear suave, collected and super confident even cold when they are dealing with the most beautiful women, which to onlookers doesn't make sense because it's too far out of their realities-something they could never, ever imagine doing themselves!

One reason why they're able to do this is because they've got too much on their plates, limited energies and time to really care of any one target! It's far easier to replace than stick and try to work it out with troublesome prospects. There are literally tons of that where it came from and each one can easily be replaced within a minute or two if so desired.

Abundance Mentality

Having an abundance of anything makes the individual pieces means far less noteworthy than it would otherwise be. When someone is acting special trying to leverage off her rarity and high status? This is the antidote!

Forcing yourself to stop caring by overwhelming yourself through sheer numbers and excess! After a specific point you just lose track of the individual targets and it just becomes impossible for you to care for each and every individual thing when you've got so much of that in storage.

There is only so much caring existing around you can allocate and the mind has limited bandwidth to keep track of too many people and things all at once. It shuts down and stops caring once the thresholds have been reached.

If you knew there would be dozens, even hundreds of these

people laying around, would you actually care enough to have tunnel vision for that one so-called "special" girl?

That is one of the justifications why or how someone in this line of work can be so cold and not really give a shit about each individual target. To be frank, the problem isn't how to stop caring, but when you reach abundance and beyond? It's how to put back the caring! How to get more anxieties, how to get nervous, how to get excited and stimulated, to feel adrenaline to push you to the limits of your game and abilities!

Even the most caring people just can't care for everyone! Mother Theresa cares for everyone but there's billions of children I doubt she had enough to give to each one child.

Anyway these high-performing people need to go through a lot of targets to get good at their crafts. There's just no other way to get good except through a lot of practice and practice involves burning through a lot of leads!

This kind of mentality is adopted by a lot of people who constantly deal with many prospects on a regular basis. They are distanced emotionally until the prospect becomes useful. The agent or the operator does not lose sleep over losing any one of his gazillion prospects. Frankly it's easier to just get a new one, than fret about that one that got away. Why the heck would he care if the prospect thinks he's obnoxious, pushy or lame? It's a feat if he can even remember that prospect's name! Nothing personal, it's all business, the nature of numbers games.

A Dash of Superiority Complex

Sometimes a controlled dose of superiority doesn't hurt. Regardless of what others may think, that you come off arrogant or a snob? Who cares! True you care of their cumulative opinions or general feedback as a whole but you don't really care enough about each individual's opinions.

As politically incorrect or demeaning as it may sound, looking at others as inferiors or how a pet owner would look at his pets gives you that "unaffected, I don't give a fuck, your opinion simply doesn't matter" attitude that's very useful for our objective.
You certainly do not care about their opinions because they're your pets. They are there for your entertainment only! No different from let's say a college student being taught by a five-year-old child how to do his quantum physics assignment.

If you know everything and anything about the subject matter at hand, there is just no way you can make yourself care of the opinions voiced by inferiors who don't know anything! Talking to an inferior makes you even dumber by being fed stupid ideas and opinions.

Everything, including that attitude problem everyone despises can be made into a resource- so don't judge!

Our goal is to be unaffected and this is one way to do it effectively. How many individuals with real delusions of grandeur do you know who actually care or get affected by puny human's sentiments? It feels good to sound like a super villain hehe.
Take this advice with a grain of salt. This is a means to get you to where you want to go.

You shouldn't **really** be like them! You're just borrowing their psychology and attitudes to get a specific psychological effect! Be also aware that this reflects on your nonverbals and vibes so do your best to conceal that smug and air of superiority or else people will surely hate you!

Another mind set you could try out is recognize that you probably won't see that person ever again!! Whatever they say or think for the time being could be minorly useful to an extent but in the long run? Who cares! You're not going to see them again! The problem though is when they stay. You may need to shift to another mindset that will get it done.

The Psychopath

To be psychopathic involves being emotionally unable to care. It's a disability! You don't have the ability to feel.

You're not connected to your emotions as much as you want to because of chemical imbalances and odd hardwiring's in their brains. They like to engage in high-risk stuff that scares the bajezuz of us mere mortals, because of that deep longing to feel something-anything!

You have to find a way to get to that state. That you absolutely do not care and there's nothing that can make you care, although you want to. Again make the distinction between someone who cares too much, trying hard not to, versus someone who has a disability but wanting the opposite... He wants to care, his body is unable!

There are various gateways you can enter to get to this point or emotional state. That should be your objective: to arrive at that place when it comes to you effortlessly and naturally.

Willpower

At times we may need to allocate energy and block the caring or develop unnatural hate or disgust or use sheer willpower to stop the emotional attachments were feeling.

Because it's not organic and therefore artificial? It's just a matter of time before you break down or exhaust energy to fighting the emotions!

It's better to BE, than to just DO. Doing something tactically denotes and requires energy. Being is naturally being that sort of individual that does not care. Do you expend energy not caring what your cousin's neighbor's best friend thinks? Its effortless and requires no energy consumption. You just don't give a shit! You can be totally drunk or half asleep and you still won't care. Someone using willpower to not care will start to care once he gets tired. The energy used in fighting the emotions become depleted.

Find your motivations to get into that head space where you naturally just cant give a damn even if you wanted! You can force it by using willpower as said previously, which may work for some purpose, especially if its short term, but if we're talking long term? Using willpower won't be a good strategy! It requires too much effort and energy!

Find that space that does not require energy nor effort. It's a viable long term strategy that can sustain you. Plus the energy signature is much purer and forceful than someone trying to fake not giving a damn, when he clearly does! Look at forums and your friends' Facebook posts, you won't have to wander far, you're bound to see "I don't care" posts. Yet just by broadcasting to the world they don't care? Guess what, they actually do!

In the PUA community you also see this a lot. They don't really understand the science behind not caring or shutting off emotions. You can't just will yourself to stop caring just because you wanted to! The people who post that? I guarantee you they do care, they're just being try hard wannabes!

Not Created Equal

There are many kinds of uncaring and not all are created equal, nor serve the same purpose and fixed with the same techniques.

Not all can be learned artificially, some variants of not caring are just naturally built-in to some people who have psychopathic tendencies. We wouldn't want to adopt them anyway! Criminals, thieves, murderers and other characters without conscience get their rocks off hurting others! We don't want that I hope?

Other variants can be learned quite easily if you know how to do it and trace route why exactly you are affected by certain forces and influences in your life. The ability to be uncaring of rejections is one such variant that is absolutely desired by many. Inability to fall in love or get too emotionally attached to targets is another one.

Pleasing Others For The Sake Of Pleasing

As social creatures it's just human nature to want to please, be liked and impress our friends and family. Men especially who were born naturally competitive not only view this as absolutely necessary to impress their peers but more so to impress thaaa ladies.

It feels great to receive accolades from friends and family, especially more so when the praises come from the people we respect and look up to. Social rankings are also established by our achievements and opinions from our peers and superiors. We grew up in tribes and social circles which means our ranks or positions are determined by their valuations of us. We care what people think for a reason!

This is a survival mechanism.

Deep down as social creatures we want to that sense of belongingness, love and respect from the tribes we belong to Some of us may not be consciously aware of it, but its influence is exerted in all of the things we do. We overhype our war stories, we brag about things we've done or possess, we try to present a better version of ourselves because of desire for the above.

World Realities Versus Your Own Reality

Do numbers affect truth? If 5 people believed the world is round while the opposition numbering in the millions believed it's actually triangular, does the belief of the majority make it truth?

Human beings tend to make it so. The more popular an opinion is, the more real it tends to be at least in terms of perception by the vast majority.

If you believe you're the shit, and 100 people were paid by a jealous friend to convince you that those 100 people believe you're scum of the earth? How would that affect the belief of the only person who believes in you? The one opinion that matters the most.
If you don't believe in your greatness, no one else will!

Having majority vote on what is supposedly real does not make it any more or less true.

It just reinforces the illusion that we forget we're enveloped in all of the time. That we got accustomed to living like this in the world. It is just a shortcut how all humans think about things and over the course of time we forget the map is not the territory. From reality itself, there is a filter of subjective perception, a buffer if you will, but we forget it even exists. We mistakenly assume we're directly operating in reality!

If you want to destroy their sense of self-worth and identity? Try to get as many people buy into the idea you're proposing against that person's perception of himself. The more you can convince that person that what he thinks about himself is inaccurate and by creating enough loopholes to cause him to question himself. By creating a compelling case and providing believable enough proof to your assertions? Couple that with a bunch of people agreeing with you? That would destroy what he used to think to be real. Or at least create enough questions in his mind to demoralize him!

Isn't that what happens to us naturally without anyone necessarily masterminding the destruction of our self-esteems?

There is absolute reality which is free of subjective analysis and just is the way it is without any labels! There is consensual reality which is what functions in normal life where we determine what is real based on the number of people holding the same beliefs. Unless something is deserving of closer scrutiny where we put time and energy to proving or disproving it through research, experiments etc.

Personal Bubble

Someone suffering from Autism or Aspergers have traits about them that make it easy for them to live in their own personal bubbles, shielded from the world. We can learn a thing or two that we can emulate, atleast to lessen our caring for the external world.

It we're to reverse engineer how personal bubbles work to shield us from the outside world? It boils down to not referencing externally and putting our focus inside! Imagine you are Ironman moving and perceiving the world not directly outside, but only through the suit and the images produced internally with its high-tech display units and monitors.

Do you think any person inside the suit is as sensitive to the outside world without it? Directly perceiving the world with his naked senses, unpadded by the suit?

There is an added layer of protection and buffering that makes him feel more protected, disconnected and isolated from the rest of the world.

If you had the same suit, but is transparent and no one else **can** see it? Do you think it would make you a little more confident and less sensitive to what others are thinking? If you wanted to be in asshole, wouldn't it be easier if you were wearing a transparent iron man's suit or without it?

In theater acting especially they use masks to bring out certain persona and be another person. Such is the power of masks! Would you be the same if you were wearing one of those mission impossible disguises allowing you to look like anyone and whatever you say and do is inconsequential because you're doing it under an anonymous persona?

The Bufferzone

When I first got into the stuff more than a decade ago, trying to be desensitized to the world, I had my first brush with the Star Trek world and modeled the emotionally distant trait of Tuvak, an officer of the Starship Voyager.

Tuvak was of the Vulcan race. Vulcans in the Star Trek universe were once highly emotional, raw, primal beings who destroyed themselves because of their inability to control their emotions. One of their ancestors founded a movement of emotional suppression and pure logic which later saved their entire race!

You can do the same and deliberately try to repress your emotions and create the *one second buffer* between that emotion and your reaction to the emotion. Most people don't recognize that buffer exists!

You don't have to feel the way you do after the emotional stimulus. Recognize that one second exists from the cause of the emotion to the reaction. That will set you on your way to mindfully controlling how you're going to react to the stimulus.

Logic works when you are not enslaved like an animal- not having intellectual choice on how you're going to react emotionally to a stimulus. Stimulus-response to them is literally instantaneous! They don't have the faculty of logic to aid them. That buffer doesn't exist.

You can further maintain your power over the stimulus-response reaction by prolonging that buffer. For example someone spat on your face so you get angry ofcourse and want to kill him. More and more practice extending the one second to two seconds to five seconds etc.will give you more control of your animalistic outbursts.

I am not a fan of pure emotional suppression myself but extending the buffer zone does work.

Social Conditioning

Another one of the determinants of our self-image or identity is societal conditioning. This includes popular media and what we consider to be the beginning formative essays we heard from our childhood friends, teachers and parents which were instrumental in forming our initial self-images. That day was the starting point we started having conceptual definitions of who we believe we were. People around us serving as our mirrors, making us see ourselves through their eyes, which may or may not be accurate and for sure subject to strong bias.

In our formative years we naturally had to depend on not only on our parents and guardians but also with our peers and seniors to make us understand about life and the world. How did you first developed that self-image and where did it come from? Did you start life already knowing who you were? Did you read it off some book? Everyone's opinion of himself of course came from the people surrounding him! Well until he finally understood and found out who he really was!

They defined our self-concepts. As children we were not fortified or defended against damaging ideas as to who we were. If you come from a nurturing environment then you're lucky you'll have a good self-image growing up. If you come from an abusive background? You carry those insecurities and damage all your life unless they get fixed at some point.

Know Thyself

Sometimes it's no longer simply about knowing more! Everyone knows more about themselves than anyone else ! Except why do we care about others opinions of us? It doesn't make sense at all! Even if you could be presented with unquestionable proof of your high status you'll still have doubts if you're not really secured within yourself. You can see this behavior with the most beautiful women even to those who still insist on getting cosmetic surgeries done on their faces even though most people think they're goddesses!

They may have tremendous proof that indeed they are exceptionally beautiful beings and yet somehow can find reasons to be insecure? How does one learn to become insecure when you already have everything? It doesn't make sense doesn't it? And that is why you have to know thyself more than anyone else and learn specifically about your weaknesses (including redeeming qualities) and why do you really care too much?

Is it because of a weak self esteem? Is it an identity crisis because you don't know who you are yet? Or you do know you are but you are just constantly insecure for no apparent reason!

Caring about external opinion says more about you than about them giving their predictable opinions.

Caring too much or "externally referencing" is an indication of being unsure in oneself. If don't know yourself well enough, or you don't feel entitled to it, you have to constantly ask for reference externally. Self seeking behaviors as they are called, because you seek your identity based off the opinion of others! If you know something extremely well inside and out there is no point why you would even care at all about tertiary opinions about something they may not know that well about.

You are the authority who knows the subject best and every fact of the situation. Ultimately if you want to stop caring then you just have to organically stop caring! Being in that place where caring is almost impossible and absurd!

Why Do You Care Again?

Caring about something too much indicates as mentioned earlier an irrational fear of loss of something of value you already possess or may possibly get in the near future. Your unconscious mind wants to preserve the status quo. With good intentions it thinks it's trying to protect you in spite of the possibility of future gains when you take this gamble. That is just how the unconscious mind works. It may want to protect you by making you feel good or bad feelings that preserve or threaten your survival and replication values.

Another important distinction is the unconscious mind thinks simplistically and sometimes illogical and stupid even. It only understands preservation of value even if at the price of massive gains!

All it understands is to keep you safe because you've been kept alive up until now, it thinks what you've been doing so far has been working well (you're alive aren't you?) so why fix something that ain't broke?

It's part of its core programming to actually prevent you from engaging in higher risk activities although it may result to positive outcomes eventually.
It needs to preserve its self by any means and like other subconscious messages, for us to take it seriously it utilizes strong emotions to control us! Logic maybe on our side, we know they are safe and potentially valuable, yet we fear them nonetheless.

For example when you see an attractive girl, obviously bored and alone, the logical and smart thing to do is make the approach! Even if you've done this thousands of times, you'll still feel the approach anxiety virtually every time! Why fear something that makes absolutely no sense? In order to exercise dominion the subconscious uses emotions , fears and other intimidation tactics to control you!

It makes you care too much of potential rejections and other scenarios that may unlikely happen, and if it does? So what, you're a bigboy you can handle it! The conscious mind doesn't see it that way. It just hates risk like the plague!

The unconscious mind is designed simply to guide you through the use of emotions that you can't ignore. By making you gravitate towards things that it thinks are good for you to increase your survivability and replication values while making you afraid of things that threaten it! Sometimes there's a direct clash making you super excited and desiring to approach while producing fear factors that stop you! Why doesn't it just make up its mind?

The unconscious mind works simplistically as mentioned earlier, anything that could potentially increase or decrease the value of our S&R will feel good or threatening, sometimes even both!
People naturally either become intimidated or gravitate towards people of a higher S&R values to them. We want to align with them or get threatened by them, depends on your initial assessment and intuition.

You've finally succeeded in making this gorgeous supermodel agree to go on a date with you. You run into a friend who happens to be with Colin Farrell! Your friend asks if you guys want to be introduced to him…what would you feel?

On the one hand the tremendous Survival and social value Colin can add to your life if he finds you cool to hangout with or perhaps become interested in stuff you're marketing etc. On the other hand he's way too high value and attractive, your supermodel date is for sure going to be attracted to him! You stand no chance!

Do you want to increase your Survival value by aligning to him, or protect your Replication value potential by ensuring she doesn't get stolen by him!

We are naturally hardwired as a survival mechanism to naturally be guided by our emotions in this way so that we know who to align with or who to watch out for.

Ego

The thing is ego isn't real! It's just a collection of pictures and concepts that we mistakenly think to be the same as the core and true us!. An animal has no ego, it cannot form a mental idea of itself. It can only form limited self-concepts just enough to be alive.

The ego tries to preserve the status quo by giving you an update on the highs and lows and other changes in status. Humans naturally move through the world of metrics and gauging where we measure things and their relation to us!

It keeps us safe and know where we are at all times-like a gps. It is useful and practical even necessary! What becomes damaging is when you forget what is important and base everything on ego based measurements and valuations. When we forget It's not real and at anytime we can choose to disconnect should we desire it.

Ego Feeding Frenzy

The idea of an ego feeding frenzy means you are feeding the ego with anything that hypes up its perceived values. Anytime you receive praises, achieve an accomplishment, anything at all that make you feel special? It inflates your positive self-image or ego positively. The more it gets, the more it wants! Every time you do the exact opposite and breakdown your self-concept negatively you'll feel awful.

It is our sense of existence, the sense of "I" is how the ego appears to us. The ego is not the same as self-esteem.

Self-esteem Versus Ego

Self-esteem is invisible, it is not a necessarily a mental concept. How not to give a fuck and anything that affects your ego, your survival and replication value also affects your emotions. This is hardwired into all of us. It make us feel bad things that threaten us, while giving us good feelings if it helps our survival and replication values.

Self-esteem need not be connected to other's opinions nor to what you have achieved or possess in the world. As we get older and become conditioned to respond to these influences from people and the environment? We forget about pure self-esteem, minus the materialisms and cause and effects!

*Ego thinking is: I think/feel I am X **because** of Y.*
Self esteem is: I think/feel X because I friggin said so! There is no because, it just is.
In this bar I am the most attractive.
In this office, I am the most intelligent.

It doesn't have to be true necessarily, you just have to believe and feel it, atleast in that short duration of time.

The children exists in pure self-esteem. They have no concept of measurements and partitions yet. They don't give a shit, they just want to do what they want!

They don't care if you're the friggin president, the kid will talk to you if he wants to! He doesn't know about status, social rankings, entitlements, S&R values yet. He doesn't know you're not supposed to do XYZ and you're supposed to do ABC in some. They're operating from pure self esteem, not necessarily confident, just indifferent, still uncontaminated by societal conditionings and programming on what to think, believe, say and do in modern society.

They are the living embodiments of not giving a shit!

Conclusions

Congratulations for having reached this point. You should now have a better understanding of the mechanisms and forces why you care when you shouldn't.

There is sufficient clues and keywords provided here should you want to deepen your training.

If you read my other materials, you'd realize I'm big on emotional discharging in combination with mental installations.

Mental installations require training and experience however emotional discharging is relatively easy to do by a layman and quite powerful! A simple search on Google will provide you enough information how to do this.

But these are only pieces of the puzzle. Some problems may require complete re-indoctrination or changing of your beliefs and values about that specific thing.

As with anything, the more you practice and gain experience the better you get at it!

I would also like to point out that anything fresh and new is more emotionally stimulating than something you've done many times.

We may all get extremely excited by getting several hundred bucks to a few thousand dollars. If that becomes your daily reality? Like rags to riches entrepreneurs and musicians? From shock to excitement it becomes ho-hum nonevents eventually.

So get more experience and be desensitized to things that still give you highly emotional reactions.
Let's say you are afraid of rejections? Deliberately go out and be rejected dozens of times-and we do this just so you know-and just like magic watch as it completely disappears without a trace!

This guide is not intended as and may not be construed as an alternative to or a substitute for professional mental counseling, therapy or medical services and advice.

The authors, publishers, and distributors of this guide have made every effort to ensure the validity, accuracy, and timely nature of the information presented here. However, no guarantee is made, neither direct nor implied, that the information in this guide or the techniques described herein are suitable for or applicable to any given individual person or group of persons, nor that any specific result will be achieved. The authors, publishers, and distributors of this guide will be held harmless and without fault in all situations and causes arising from the use of this information by any person, with or without professional medical supervision. The information contained in this book is for informational and entertainment purposes only. It not intended as a professional advice or a recommendation to act.

No part of this book may be reproduced or transmitted in any form whatsoever, electronic, or mechanical, including photocopying, recording, or by any informational storage or retrieval system without express permission from the author.

© Copyright 2013, Jack N. Raven
Date of Creation 12/17/2013
All rights reserved.

ABOUT THE AUTHOR

Jack N. Raven finished AB Legal Management and MBA-Management. He has studied many areas of applied Psychology, Manipulation and Persuasion such as Hypnosis, Neuro-Linguistic Programming (equivalent Practitioner and Master Practitioner training level), Tradecraft, Sales, Marketing, Copywriting, Seduction (Practically having studied and experienced and gotten success with beautiful women in all major systems available i.e. Natural, Indirect, Direct, SS systems etc; Sedona Method ™, Emotional Freedom Techniques™. He has over a decade of experience and training in esoteric systems like Qi-Gong, Bardon Hermetics, Keylontic Sciences, Quantum Touch ™ and other energy healing systems.

He has studied various martial arts and miscellaneous self improvement systems and technologies.

His current passion is Digital Arts and Fashion Photography.

If you have any questions please LIKE and PM me at my facebook.

http://www.facebook.com/jacknraven

Other books by Jack N. Raven Publishing

The Seduction Force Multiplier 1- Bring Out Your FULL Seduction powers through
the Power of Routines, Drills, Scripting and Protocols

This is book #1 and a must read if you are serious in exploring and maximizing your seduction potential. Includes more in depth information on how to construct, internalize and the advantages of Scripting versus Natural game convos.

The Seduction Force Multiplier 2 - Scripts and Routines Book

This is the main routines manual which contains the full lines and routines, that are shortened in this book. More than 700 of them!

Also includes the full audio of the routines you can listen to.

The Seduction Force Multiplier 3- PUA Routines Memory Transplant Package

This is book #3 that includes nearly 2 hours of audio. A one of a kind system that allows you to easily memorize about 700 routines and lines from book #2, in just days!

Imagine the dramatic improvements in your game, if you can internalize hundreds of routines! Routines you wont have a problem summoning. All on muscle memory, reflexive, ready to go, just automatically flows out of your mouth without effort in the field!

The Seduction Force Multiplier 4 - Situational PUA Scripts and Routines

In this book, specific routines or scripts have been made focusing on the most common scenarios facing the PUAs.
These are specific game recipes exactly made covering that particular environment or situation! From opening to mid-game, everything is handed to you.

The Seduction Force Multiplier V - Target Auto Response Package

This book covers over 160 target/set reactions so you wont have to rack your brains coming up with responses, and so you can handle each reaction effectively!

Over 900 lines covering 160 reactions so you won't have to rack your brains coming up with effective responses.
Also includes methods to INTERNALIZE/MEMORIZE the material.

Jack N. Raven

The Seduction Force Multiplier VI - PUA Innergame, Mindsets and Attitudes

THis book contains the helpful mindsets proven succesful by thousands of PUAs, veteran and rookies. These are the missing pieces to an already powerful outergame repertoire.
Also contained in the book: how to game JEDI, or nonverbally, allowing you to be whoever you want to be!

Not only in terms of improving your seduction powers, it will also help you become not only solid on the outside, but rock solid from within!

Jack N. Raven

Shielded Heart - How To Stop Yourself From Falling For A Seduction Target

For one reason or another you probably don't want to fall in love for that girl or guy. This book is the only book of its kind dealing with this sensitive subject! This will make you invulnerable to strong feelings, in order for you to not fall for a seduction target.

How To Cheat Proof Your Relationships

A thought provoking book, entirely about the subject of seducing someone in a relationship! Either as the aggressor/Player, or the lover wanting to protect his or her love from being seduced by 3rd party Operators and Seducers.

Secrets to Hacking Your Brain- Be Your Own Therapist

A book on the best techniques from various self help disciplines like NLP, Hypnosis, EFT etc, on how to remove any feelings, and emotions at will!

Hypno Machines - How To Convert Every Object In Your Environment As a Device For Psychological and Emotional Manipulator

Based on the NLP principle of Anchoring, this book will allow you to convert literally everything that exists in the world, as your change agents, that work automatically in the background creating emotional and psychological developments and changes.

The same concept can be used in persuasion too, if you are inclined.

The Art Of Virtual Practice 2 - Learning and Mastery Of Any Skill At Lighting Speeds!

It takes about 10,000 hours to be a MASTER at any craft. By following the techniques on this book? You can cut that that to a fraction of the time!

You can get more field time/practice time by doing these special techniques-anytime, anywhere! Imagine any skill, you can learn to master it at a fraction of the time!

How to Operate with Your Full Potential and Talents

If you've always wanted to perform at your 100% best but couldn't? Then this is for you!

By figuring out your deepest motivations and "why"s, every part of what you're doing becomes more charged, solid, and FORCEFUL!

You will feel energized, centered, and fully aligned with your full powers, talents and capabilities! Alignment is the key to unlocking your full potential!

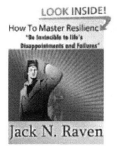

How To Master Resilience And Be Invincible To Life's Disappointments And Failures

By developing the proper mindsets, and seeing what these negative, hurtful energies for what they truly are? The reader can strengthen his fortitude, and almost enjoy failures, as a means of reaching the higher levels!

And no, this book won't tell you to live in a fairy tale world, and stay positive all the time!

The X-Factor Manual - Learn How To be A Model Even If You Don't Look Like One

A book for increasing sex appeal, though written with models in mind? The principles and techniques also apply to regular men and women, who want to increase attractiveness using modeling techniques, as well as techniques from other disciplines.

The Age Erase System - Hypnotic Anti Aging Serum

You don't have to settle with getting old. Just with the power of your mind, you can reverse the ravaging effects of time on your health, organs, skin and even looks!

Try this for a month, and tell me it doesn't work! I dare you!

Develop Insane Self Confidence and Naturally Unleash The Supermodel Within

This program will allow you to unleash the hidden gorgeous creature hiding inside of you. This program will easily unleash, in no time at all, your sexy self confidence and sex appeal.
Field tested to give you absolute results!

The Persuaders Guide To Eliminating Resistance And Getting Compliance

If you are a Persuader (who isn't), this book can teach you how to navigate and make your offers to minimize, even eliminate resistance from subjects/targets!

If you can master resistance? You can master persuasion!

The Art of Invisible Compliance - How To Make People Do What You Want Effortlessly

This book includes the Ins and Outs of making people do what you want, as covertly or overtly as you want.
If you've wondered how Intelligence Operatives make people do things short of coercion, this is how they do it.

The principles work in any persuasion setting, whether seduction, sales, marketing, anything that involves getting a desired action(compliance) from people. This book will teach you how to move INVISIBLY to get what you want, without revealing your position yourself! Very useful for covert persuasions.

Unstoppable and Fearless - Know What You Want and Get It

By knowing what you want, you now need the courage to actually get it and win! This book explores and gives you practical steps how you can reduce the fears, and make you unusually comfortable with fears and places outside your comfort zones.

Just Go- Having The Courage and Will to Pursue Your Dreams

Most people are afraid to go after what they want, let alone actually pursue it! This book will help to set you on your way!

How To Make Better Life Decisions

This book will help you to make crucial life decisions in every facet of life!

It helps give you the tools and elements to consider in weighing the many possible courses of actions and alternatives, to help you choose the absolute best decisions each and every time!

How To Diet Like a Machine- Make Any Diet Program Work With Ease

This book will give you the tools to PERMANENTLY brainwash yourself to loving the new diet meal program. You'll hate it in the beginning, but you'll grow to love it!
Because everyone hates diets, and the only way a sane person will want to keep it, is if gets reprogrammed forcefully!

Friends into Lovers: Escape and Never be Trapped In The Friendzone Ever Again!

If you're currently trapped or would like to be un-trapped in this dreaded zone now and in the future? You absolutely must check out the information in this book. Some people are born almost to be forever categorized in this zone, while others just seem to have "it", they can't get friendzoned if they wanted! This book will show you how to solve this problem-PERMANENTLY!

The Permanent Anti-jealousy Solution

This ugly poison of an emotion destroys relationships, be constantly hurt by cold-hearted players, even destroy self-esteem! Just what is "jealousy" and how do we make it disappear?

By the end of reading this book, you'll be leaving with specific tools to achieve exactly that! By understanding what is jealousy, you'll be protected against its ill effects while having the power to create this effect on targets! You'll also catch a glimpse how we get victimized using this powerful emotion.

The TEN Game Operations Manual: How To Get Extremely Gorgeous 10s Consistently and Predictably!

Most Seduction Gurus and systems ignore the existence of 10 game. Most PUAs or Seducers will never get 10s until the end of their seduction careers because seduction systems are designed for regular girls! The 10s require specialized game, without knowing these secrets? Be part of the statistics!

How Not To Give a Shit!: The Art of Not Caring

Would you like to learn how to stop giving a damn?There are situations where you just need to remove emotional attachments to people and situations to function properly.

In this book we go into great detail on the forces why we care (when this is not a luxury), and how we can dismantle these elements effectively! To liberate ourselves from caring too much, stop caring what others think-to make us emotionally detached!

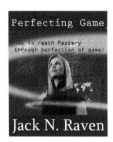

Perfecting Your Game: How To Reach Mastery Through Perfection Of Game!

This book is all about improving your performance in your chosen industry/game/craft/sport and reaching master class as quickly as humanly possible! It contains ideas where to get more tools, more powers to enhance your performance and maximize the performance you're getting from the existing ones, without having to add anything new.

Manipulative Eye Contact Techniques: Install thoughts and feelings just with your eyes!

This book will teach you powerful, easy, and covert techniques that will give you the power to "suggest" or install any thought, picture, feelings to any target, any time!

Made in the USA
Middletown, DE
14 July 2020